THINK FACTORY:
AMAZING INVENTIONS

BY MELVIN AND GILDA BERGER

D1275113

For Jacob, our dear "teknoboi," B & Z

CONTENTS

THE BIG THREE

4 INVENTIONS THAT CHANGED THE WORLD

6 COMPUTERS

8 LASERS

10 TRANSISTORS

KEEPING IN TOUCH

12 RADIOS

14 TELEVISIONS

16 CELL PHONES

18 COMPACT DISCS

GETTING AROUND

20 AUTOMOBILES

22 AIRPLANES

24 HELICOPTERS

26 ROCKETS

FIGHTING DISEASE

28 ANTIBIOTICS

30 X-RAYS

32 GENETIC ENGINEERING

MAKING LIFE EASIER

34 PLASTICS

36 ROBOTS

38 COPYING MACHINES

40 AIR CONDITIONERS

42 MICROWAVE OVENS

44 VACUUM CLEANERS

46 ...AND DON'T FORGET:

ROLLERBLADES

VELCRO

WIRE COAT HANGERS

FRISBEES

BALLPOINT PENS

INVENTIONS THAT CHANGED THE WORLD

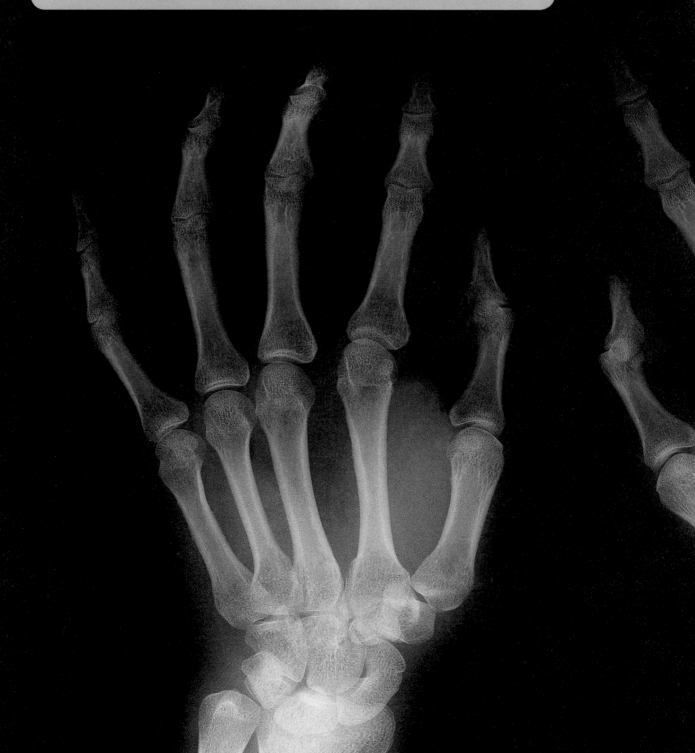

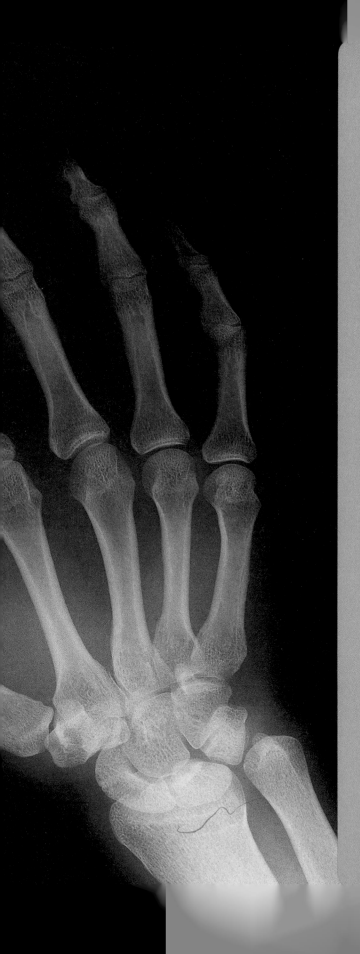

Suppose you woke up one morning and found yourself back in the year 1900. You would find the world a very different place from the world of today.

The world of 1900 had no computers. No one traveled by automobile, airplane, or helicopter. A trip to the next town by horse and buggy could take a day. Travel from California to New York might last a week or more. A trip to the moon was a pipe dream before the invention of the rocket.

No one had a radio or a television. It took days or weeks to find out what was happening in Washington, D.C., or in other places around the world.

People died of common infections because there were no antibiotics. Doctors failed to diagnose many illnesses because there were few X-rays and no CAT scans.

Life was harder without plastics, microwave ovens, and vacuum cleaners. You sweated in summer without air conditioners and froze in winter without central heating. There was no Velcro or ballpoint pens, Rollerblades or Frisbees. Not even one wire coat hanger was to be had in the world of 1900!

COMPUTERS

THE BIG THREE

Inventors: J. Presper Eckert, Jr., and John William Mauchly Year: 1946 Country: United States

AN AMAZING MACHINE

A computer is a "thinking" machine. You feed it information called data. The computer sorts or stores the data according to a set of instructions, or commands. Finally, the computer presents the results on a screen or paper, or sends them to another machine. It does all this at high speed, without getting tired, without making a mistake, and without stopping for a snack!

THE FIRST COMPUTER

In 1946, J. Presper Eckert, Jr. and John William Mauchly built the first all-purpose, all-electronic computer. They called it ENIAC (Electronic Numerical Integrator And Computer). The purpose was to make army weapons more accurate. But ENIAC didn't just sit on a desk or a lap. The computer, which was 10 feet (3 m) tall and weighed 30 tons (33 t), filled a huge room! ENIAC could do 5,000 additions in a second. (Computers today are about two million times faster!)

FAST AND SMART

Computers are fast because they have almost no moving parts. They operate on tiny pulses of electricity that zip through the computer. Computers are "smart" because they have great memories. One part of the memory holds the commands, while another part holds the data. The memory of one computer, for example, can hold the entire collection of a huge library!

THE INTERNET

The Internet is a worldwide system of linked computers. On the Internet, you can gather information, send e-mails, chat with friends, or shop. The Internet was set up by the U.S. Department of Defense in 1969.

COMPUTERS AT WORK

People use computers for everything—from writing school reports to forecasting the weather. Computers control satellites and the engines of cars, planes, and trains. You find them in CD and DVD players, digital wristwatches, video cameras, microwave ovens, air conditioners, and TVs. It's hard to imagine a world without computers!

LASERS

Inventor: Theodore H. Maiman Year: 1960 Country: United States

ON THE BEAM

A laser is a sharp, narrow, powerful beam of light. The word *laser* is made up of the first letters of Light Amplification by Stimulated Emission of Radiation. Laser light is not like light from the sun or a lightbulb, which spreads out in all directions. Lasers shine in only one direction — producing an incredibly strong form of light.

THE FIRST LASER

In 1960, Theodore H. Maiman flashed a short burst of ordinary light into a rod of synthetic ruby. The ruby had thin mirrors on either end. Inside the ruby, the mirrors bounced the light waves back and forth, making them stronger and stronger. Soon a thin, intense beam of red light burst through one end of the rod. It was the first laser!

LIGHT IS ENERGY

All light is a form of energy that travels in waves. The waves in ordinary light have different lengths and move at different speeds. They are like a crowd of people spreading out as they leave a football stadium. But laser light is different. The waves are all the same length and move together. Laser light is more like a marching band leaving the stadium all together and marching in step.

KEEPING IN TOUCH

Laser light now carries TV and radio programs, telephone calls, and computer data over great distances. Scientists change sounds, pictures, and data into a code of on/off signals. They send the signals through long, thin fiber-optic cable at nearly the speed of light. Computers at the other end change the signals back into the original sounds, pictures, or data. A fiber-optic cable can carry thousands of telephone calls and radio and TV programs at one time.

MAKING THE CUT

A laser beam as wide as a hair produces a tiny point of very hot light. Surgeons use this energy to perform surgery on the eye and other parts of the body. As the doctor moves the laser, it makes a clean, sharp cut. At the same time, its heat seals the blood vessels and stops any bleeding.

TRANSISTORS

Inventors: John Bardeen, Walter Brattain, William Shockley Year: 1947 Country: United States

SWITCH ON, SWITCH OFF

A transistor is a tiny electronic device that controls the flow of electricity. The device either turns an electric current on or off, or builds up the current. This invention is used in all electronic machines, from computers to TVs. In some ways transistors are like traffic cops. They can let traffic flow. They can stop traffic. Or they can urge drivers to move closer together so more traffic can get through.

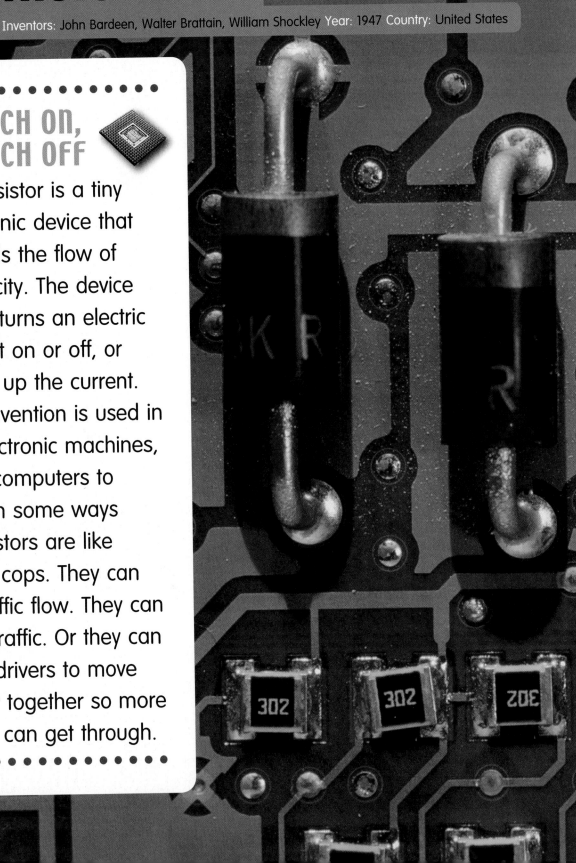

SEMICONDUCTORS

John Bardeen, Walter Brattain, and William Shockley invented the transistor in 1947. They first tested the invention on Christmas Eve that year. Transistors are built of silicon, a material that is made from sand. Silicon is a semiconductor. It falls between a good conductor of electricity like copper wire and a nonconductor like wood. Semiconductors are useful because they can stop or boost the flow of electricity.

TEENY, TINY CHIPS

Most modern electronic devices need lots of transistors. Some computers need millions. Since the invention of transistors, scientists have worked to make them smaller and smaller. Today, thousands and thousands of transistors can fit on a small flat chip of silicon no bigger than your thumbnail!

CHEAPER BY THE DOZEN

Transistors must be made in super-clean factories. Any speck of dirt can ruin them! The first transistors were manufactured in 1952. Each one cost $180. By the following year, they were smaller, cheaper, and worked better. By 1955, the price had dropped to 99¢. Now, transistors cost just pennies each.

PARTNERS

The radio and the transistor seem made for each other. For years after the radio was invented in 1894, it was big and heavy, used lots of electricity, and often broke down. Transistors changed all that. They helped make radios smaller, lighter, and much more reliable. They also made possible portable radios powered by batteries.

RADIOS

Inventor: Guglielmo Marconi Year: 1894 Country: Italy

HEAR THIS

Radio sends sounds from one place to another through the air—not through wires. Microphones in the radio studio first change speech, music, or other sounds into radio waves. These waves go to an antenna that sends them out through the air. Your home radio has a receiver that picks up the waves and changes them back to the sounds you hear.

MICROPHONE AMPLIFIER TRANSMITTER RADIO

A BOLD IDEA

Guglielmo Marconi is credited with the invention of the radio, or "wireless." But he based some of his ideas on the work of others. Two scientists, Joseph Henry and Michael Faraday, found that a current in one wire can produce a current in another wire — even though the wires are not connected. In 1894, Marconi used this idea to turn on a buzzer 30 feet (9.1 m) away. It was the first wireless, or radio, message.

MAKING WAVES

In its early days, people mostly used radio to communicate with ships at sea. But in the 1920s, home radios became very popular. Families gathered around the radio to hear music, sports, comedy shows, dramas, and news. For the first time, New York baseball fans could hear what was happening in a Yankee game in Chicago — as it was happening!

AM AND FM RADIO

The first radio stations sent out AM (Amplitude Modulation) radio waves. These waves vary in height. Later, some radio stations sent out FM (Frequency Modulation) radio waves. FM waves vibrate at different speeds. AM radio broadcasts can be received farther from the station than FM can. But FM radio has a better sound quality.

TELEVISIONS

Inventor: Vladimir K. Zworykin Year: 1929 Country: United States

HEAR AND SEE THIS

Television uses cameras and microphones to change sounds and pictures into a pattern of radio signals. Engineers send the signals out through the air or through cables. They beam some signals up to satellites, which bounce them back to TV dish antennas on Earth. TV receivers then change the signals—from the air, from cables, or from satellites—back to the original sounds and pictures.

THREE GIANT STEPS

The invention of television came in three giant steps. First, Paul Nipkow (Germany), Charles F. Jenkins (United States), and John Logie Baird (Scotland) built simple, early machines. Baird, for example, made his out of darning needles, wood, string, and glass from an old bicycle light. Philo T. Farnsworth (United States) designed an all-electrical television. Finally, in 1929, Vladimir K. Zworykin built the first modern, practical electronic TV.

FAR OUT

Television stations beam TV signals up to satellites in outer space. The satellites strengthen the signals and bounce them back to Earth. Satellite TV dishes on Earth pick up the signals. They pass through wires to TV sets, which change the signals back to the original sounds and pictures.

A SMALL WORLD

Television helps bring people closer together. It makes the world a smaller place. Millions of people around the world now watch the same shows, laugh at the same jokes, follow the same sports teams, and listen to the same music. TV provides people worldwide with similar experiences and ways of keeping in touch.

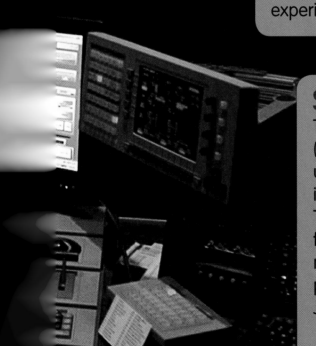

SHARPER IMAGE

The latest TV sets feature HDTV (High Definition TeleVision). HDTV uses a TV signal that carries more information than a standard signal. This gives sharper pictures with less fluttering. Ordinary TV has pictures made up of 625 lines. HDTV pictures have more than 1,000 lines! Just don't try to count them!

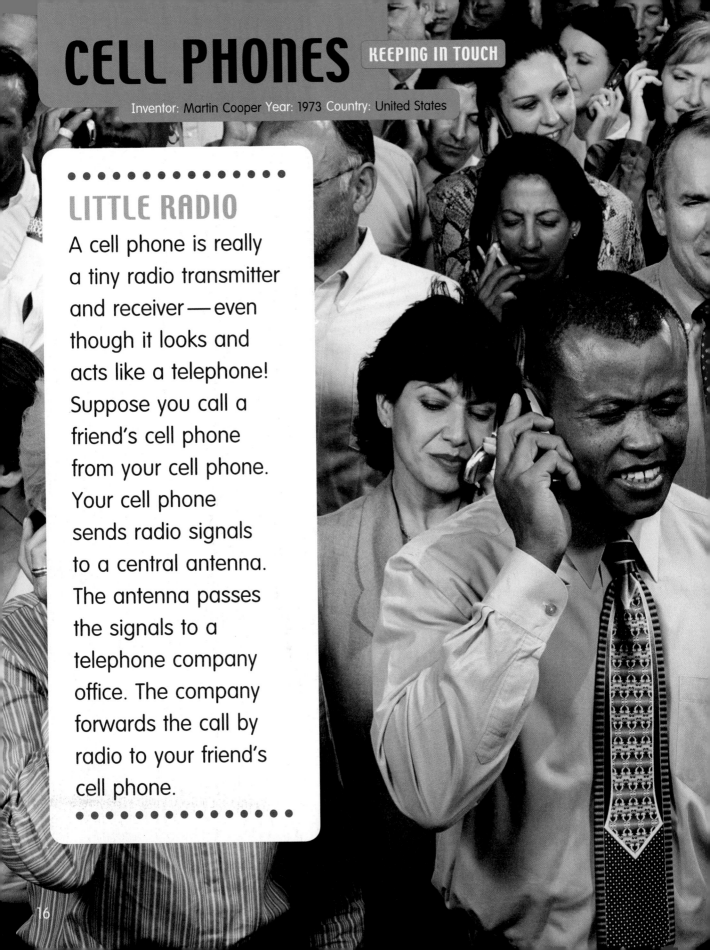

CELL PHONES

KEEPING IN TOUCH

Inventor: Martin Cooper Year: 1973 Country: United States

LITTLE RADIO

A cell phone is really a tiny radio transmitter and receiver — even though it looks and acts like a telephone! Suppose you call a friend's cell phone from your cell phone. Your cell phone sends radio signals to a central antenna. The antenna passes the signals to a telephone company office. The company forwards the call by radio to your friend's cell phone.

THE CORDLESS PHONE

Teri Pall built the first cordless phone in 1965. (She sold the invention for $2,000!) Pall's phone used a land-phone base and had a range of about 2 miles (3.2 km). But the signals reached so high that they jumbled communications between airports and low-flying airplanes! Pall then "dumbed down" (her words) the cordless phone and cut its range. The cordless phone soon became the walkie-talkie.

BATTERY PHONES

In 1973, Martin Cooper built a portable phone that was powered by batteries. This was the ancestor of the cell phone. It was a good idea. But Cooper's phone was the size of a brick and nearly as heavy. It was not something that you could slip into your pocket! Later cell phones were much smaller and better. In 1999, Randice-Lisa Altschul invented a disposable cell phone that you use for an hour and then throw away!

VERY POPULAR

Cell phones now outnumber land phones. Telephone companies have divided the country into separate parts, or cells. Each cell has its own sending and receiving antennas. When you speak on a cell phone in a moving car, the signal automatically passes from cell to cell. Callers can now use cell phones to call from almost any place on Earth to almost any other place.

THE TOP FIVE CELL-PHONE USING COUNTRIES IN THE WORLD

The United States is the country with the most cell phone users.

Country	Percentage	Users
U.S.	38%	(158 million users)
Japan	21%	(86 million users)
Germany	16%	(64 million users)
Italy	13%	(55 million users)
Great Britain	12%	(49 million users)

COMPACT DISCS

Inventor: James T. Russell Year: 1972 Country: United States

STOREHOUSE OF SOUNDS

The compact disc, or CD, has largely taken the place of the phonograph record. The CD stores sounds on its surface. One CD holds more than three times as much music as a phonograph record. Finger marks, small scratches, and water harm records but don't damage CDs. And since you play a CD with light, instead of a needle, CDs almost never wear out.

BRIGHT IDEA

James T. Russell loved music. But he didn't like the poor sound he got from his phonograph records. So he spent the years from 1965 to 1970 designing a system that could produce sound with light, instead of a phonograph needle. By 1972, Russell had created a working CD. It took ten years, though, until CDs became popular.

PITS AND LANDS

To make a CD, a performer sings into a microphone connected to a computer. The computer directs a laser to cut tiny holes (pits) on a disc. It leaves other areas (lands) flat. The pits and lands store the original sounds. The CD player spins the CD very fast. Inside, a laser beam shines on the disc. Light that hits a pit is scattered. But light that hits a land bounces back. This light falls on a device that changes it into pulses of electricity — and back to the original sounds. Happy listening!

ROUND AND ROUND WE GO

The billions of pits and lands on the CD's surface form a tight spiral. It runs from the center of the disc to the outer edge. To give the best sound, the disc slows down as it spins. When the laser shines toward the center, the disc spins about 500 times a minute. By the time the laser reaches the outside edge, the disc is spinning only 200 times a minute.

ALL IN THE FAMILY

DVDs, or Digital Versatile Disks, are close relatives of CDs. But DVDs can do much more than CDs. They can hold about seven times more information. This includes sound, still pictures, and movies. A CD-ROM is a kind of DVD that people use to load data and software into computers.

AUTOMOBILES

Inventors: Gottlieb Daimler and Karl Benz Year: 1885 Country: Germany

A SLOW START

For many years, inventors tried to build a gasoline-powered car. But the car that Gottlieb Daimler and Karl Benz built in 1885 was the first one that really worked. Still, cars were very expensive and few people bought them. In 1913, Henry Ford set up an assembly line in his auto factory. Each worker did just one job. Ford's cars took less time to make, and the price went down. Soon many ordinary folks had their own cars. President Theodore Roosevelt was the first U.S. president to ride in an automobile.

AWAY YOU GO

Automobiles get power by burning gasoline inside the engine. The burning gasoline produces a burst of hot gas. The gas pushes down on engine parts, called pistons. The pistons move up and down. They are connected by a system of rods to the wheels of the car. The moving pistons turn the car's wheels — and away you go!

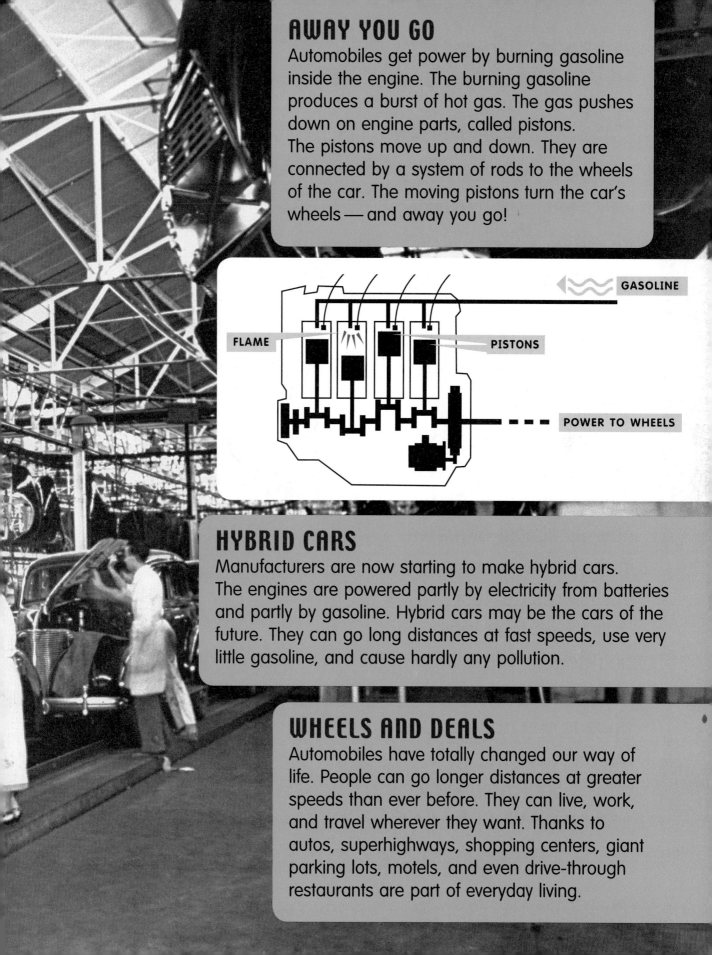

GASOLINE

FLAME

PISTONS

POWER TO WHEELS

HYBRID CARS

Manufacturers are now starting to make hybrid cars. The engines are powered partly by electricity from batteries and partly by gasoline. Hybrid cars may be the cars of the future. They can go long distances at fast speeds, use very little gasoline, and cause hardly any pollution.

WHEELS AND DEALS

Automobiles have totally changed our way of life. People can go longer distances at greater speeds than ever before. They can live, work, and travel wherever they want. Thanks to autos, superhighways, shopping centers, giant parking lots, motels, and even drive-through restaurants are part of everyday living.

AIRPLANES

Inventors: Orville and Wilbur Wright Year: 1903 Country: United States

UP, UP, AND AWAY

An airplane is a heavier-than-air flying machine. It has wings to hold it up in the air and engines to move it forward. Airplanes can carry people or cargo through the air at very high speeds. People now fly almost anywhere in the world in hours. Businesses get fast delivery on their mail and goods. Airplanes bring emergency aid to people in trouble. In war, airplanes help armies fight the enemy.

A LONG, LONG STORY

Humans have long dreamed of flying like birds. Among the first to design a flying machine with flapping wings was Leonardo da Vinci (1452–1519), the great Italian artist and inventor. Over the following centuries, many others built machines with flapping wings. Nothing worked, until people learned that the shape of the birds' wings — not the flapping — was most important!

THE WRIGHT IDEA

Orville and Wilbur Wright owned a bicycle shop in Ohio. Yet for nearly ten years they thought about building a flying machine. Finally, they built a plane made of cotton cloth over a wooden frame. It had a small gas engine that drove the two propellers. On December 17, 1903, Orville won a coin toss to become the first to fly their plane. The plane rose only 10 feet (3 m) in the air and stayed up a scant 12 seconds. But those few seconds completely changed the history of transportation!

WINGING IT

An airplane wing has the same basic shape as a bird's wing. It's flat on the bottom and curved on top. As the plane picks up speed along the ground, air rushes over the top of the wing. This air has less pressure than air passing across the bottom of the wing. The air underneath pushes up toward the air above. The push lifts up the wing and the plane takes off. In the air, the wing holds the plane up.

PULL OR PUSH

Some modern planes have propellers like the Wright brothers' plane. The front of each propeller blade is curved like the top of a plane's wing. The spinning blades lower the air pressure in front, which pulls the plane forward. Most airliners, however, get power from jet engines. Burning jet fuel produces gases that zoom out the back and push the plane forward.

HELICOPTERS

Inventor: Heinrich Focke Year: 1936 Country: Germany

WHIRLYBIRD

A helicopter is an aircraft with one or two large propellers called rotors. The rotor or rotors spin above the body of the helicopter. Most helicopters have just one rotor. The top of the rotor is curved, and the bottom is flat — just like an airplane wing. The spinning rotor holds the helicopter up in the air. By changing the angle of the rotor, the pilot moves the craft up, down, forward, backward, or sideways.

EARLY DAYS

Heinrich Focke built the first practical helicopter in 1936. It had two rotors that spun in opposite directions. This kept the craft flying straight. The female test pilot Hanna Reitsch was the first to fly Focke's helicopter. In 1939, American inventor Igor Sikorsky built a helicopter with a single rotor. To fly straight, Sikorsky had to add a small, upright propeller to the tail. The tail propeller also helped steer the helicopter.

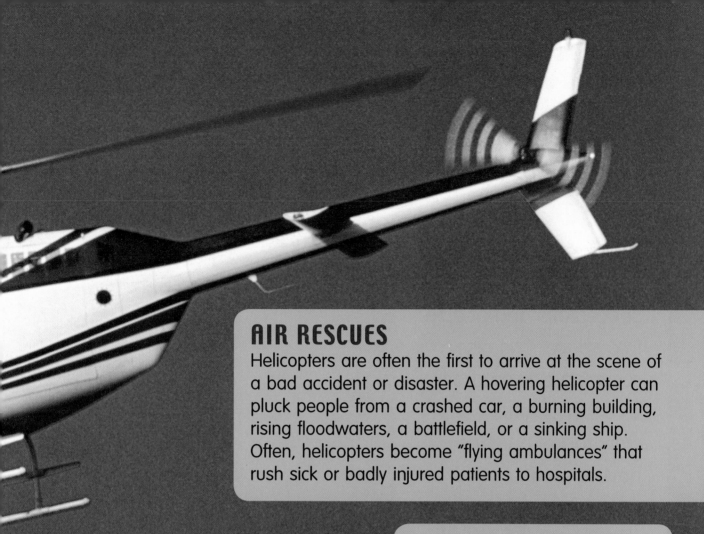

AIR RESCUES

Helicopters are often the first to arrive at the scene of a bad accident or disaster. A hovering helicopter can pluck people from a crashed car, a burning building, rising floodwaters, a battlefield, or a sinking ship. Often, helicopters become "flying ambulances" that rush sick or badly injured patients to hospitals.

PLUSES AND MINUSES

Some people think that helicopters are better than airplanes. Helicopters can hover as well as take off and land in small areas. They can also fly slower and lower than planes with wings. On the other hand, helicopters use more fuel than airplanes. Most can fly only a few hours before needing more fuel. The top speed of a helicopter is about 200 miles (320 km) per hour. That is far slower than most planes.

HARD WORKERS

Helicopters often help the police during emergencies. When police are searching for missing persons or fleeing cars, helicopters often hover above treetops, buildings, or roadways. Helicopter pilots report on traffic for radio and TV stations. Helicopters also patrol borders, track wildlife, follow migrating animals —and even deliver cargo to hard-to-reach places.

ROCKETS

Inventor: Robert Goddard Year: 1926 Country: United States

BLAST OFF

A rocket is a powerful engine that sends spacecrafts and people into space. It is also a vehicle powered by a rocket engine. Only rocket engines have enough power to break free of the earth's gravity.

Since airplane engines need to draw oxygen from air, planes cannot fly into airless space. But since rockets carry their own oxygen supply, they can go where airplanes cannot fly.

The three countries that have put the most people in space are:

U.S.	318
Russia	88
Germany	8

ROCKET POWER

Rockets date back nearly 800 years. Around that time, the Chinese began setting gunpowder on fire to shoot fireworks into the air. Much later, armies started to use rockets to shoot explosives at the enemy. In the War of 1812, the British fired rockets at American troops. That's why Francis Scott Key wrote in "The Star Spangled Banner": *And the rockets' red glare…*

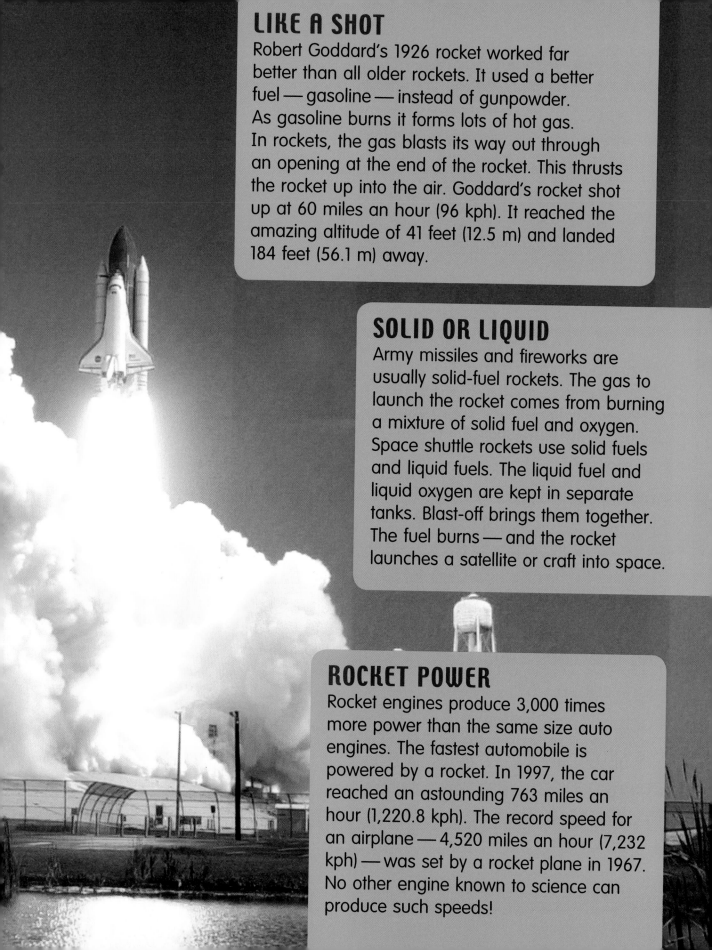

LIKE A SHOT
Robert Goddard's 1926 rocket worked far better than all older rockets. It used a better fuel — gasoline — instead of gunpowder. As gasoline burns it forms lots of hot gas. In rockets, the gas blasts its way out through an opening at the end of the rocket. This thrusts the rocket up into the air. Goddard's rocket shot up at 60 miles an hour (96 kph). It reached the amazing altitude of 41 feet (12.5 m) and landed 184 feet (56.1 m) away.

SOLID OR LIQUID
Army missiles and fireworks are usually solid-fuel rockets. The gas to launch the rocket comes from burning a mixture of solid fuel and oxygen. Space shuttle rockets use solid fuels and liquid fuels. The liquid fuel and liquid oxygen are kept in separate tanks. Blast-off brings them together. The fuel burns — and the rocket launches a satellite or craft into space.

ROCKET POWER
Rocket engines produce 3,000 times more power than the same size auto engines. The fastest automobile is powered by a rocket. In 1997, the car reached an astounding 763 miles an hour (1,220.8 kph). The record speed for an airplane — 4,520 miles an hour (7,232 kph) — was set by a rocket plane in 1967. No other engine known to science can produce such speeds!

ANTIBIOTICS

Inventor: Alexander Fleming Year: 1928 Country: England

MIRACLE DRUGS

An antibiotic is a drug. It can kill germs, or bacteria, that make people sick. Before antibiotics, doctors had few ways to kill harmful bacteria in the body. Many people died from diseases and infections that were caused by bacteria. Antibiotics are among a doctor's best tools for helping people live longer.

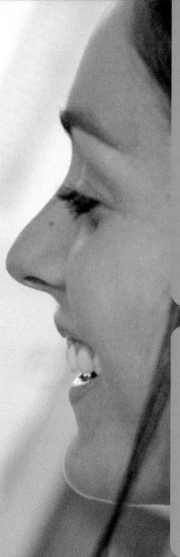

A HAPPY ACCIDENT

The first antibiotic was discovered by accident. In 1928, Dr. Alexander Fleming was growing some bacteria in his London lab. One day, he noticed a spot of green mold among the bacteria. To his surprise, he saw no live bacteria around the mold. Fleming grew more of the mold and injected it into some sick mice. He saw that the mold killed the germs but did not harm the animals. Fleming called the mold penicillin.

FIRST HUMAN PATIENT

In May 1941, a young British policeman became the first human to be treated with penicillin. The officer was near death from blood poisoning. Doctors injected him with a dose of penicillin. Sad to say, just as the patient was starting to recover, the supply of penicillin ran out, and he died.

ANTIBIOTICS AT WORK

Since Fleming's discovery, many more antibiotics have been created. They all attack bacteria without harming the body's cells. The antibiotics either kill the bacteria or stop them from growing. Antibiotics are, of course, used to treat humans. Animal doctors also use antibiotics to prevent animal diseases and to help the animals grow.

REMEMBER THIS

Penicillin and other antibiotics work against bacteria that cause disease. But they don't work against viruses. Viruses cause such diseases as colds and the flu. A doctor may give an antibiotic to someone sick with a cold or the flu. In those cases, it is to help prevent a bacterial infection.

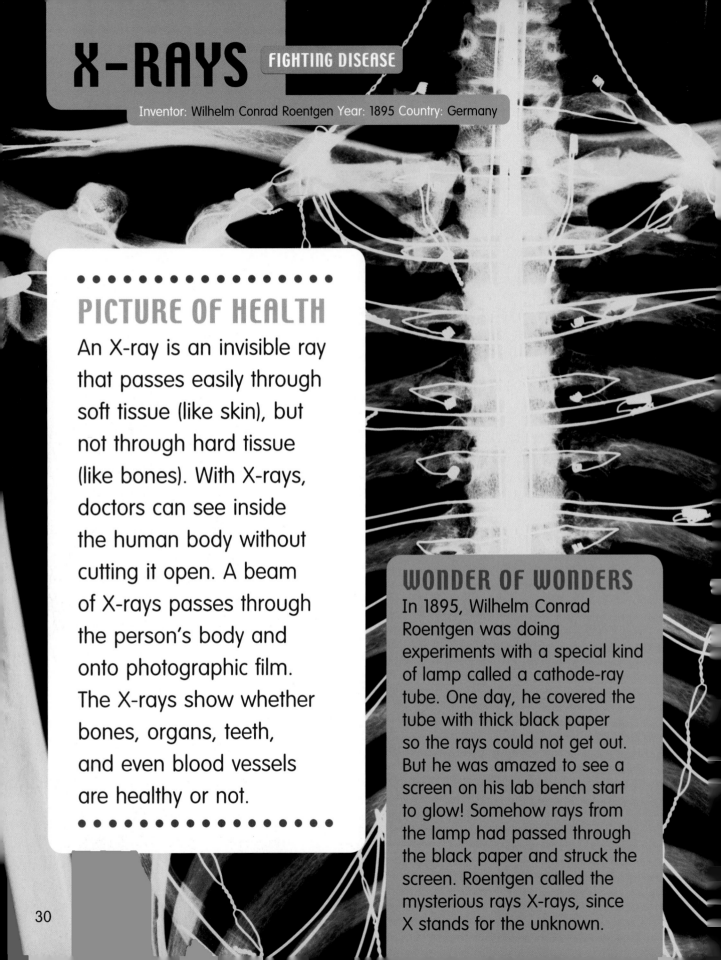

X-RAYS

Inventor: Wilhelm Conrad Roentgen Year: 1895 Country: Germany

PICTURE OF HEALTH

An X-ray is an invisible ray that passes easily through soft tissue (like skin), but not through hard tissue (like bones). With X-rays, doctors can see inside the human body without cutting it open. A beam of X-rays passes through the person's body and onto photographic film. The X-rays show whether bones, organs, teeth, and even blood vessels are healthy or not.

WONDER OF WONDERS

In 1895, Wilhelm Conrad Roentgen was doing experiments with a special kind of lamp called a cathode-ray tube. One day, he covered the tube with thick black paper so the rays could not get out. But he was amazed to see a screen on his lab bench start to glow! Somehow rays from the lamp had passed through the black paper and struck the screen. Roentgen called the mysterious rays X-rays, since X stands for the unknown.

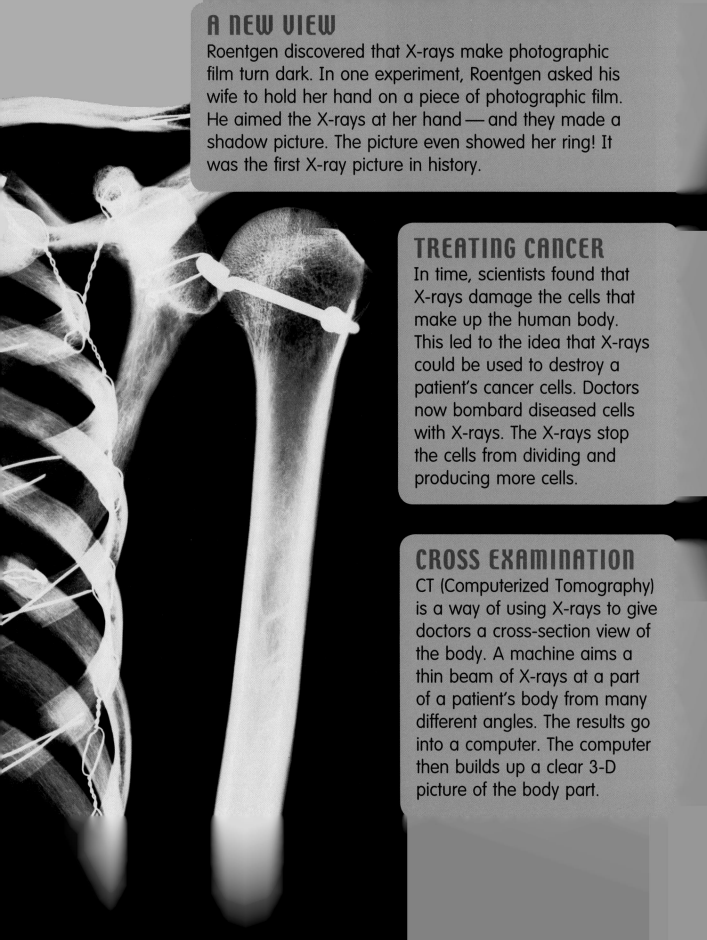

A NEW VIEW

Roentgen discovered that X-rays make photographic film turn dark. In one experiment, Roentgen asked his wife to hold her hand on a piece of photographic film. He aimed the X-rays at her hand — and they made a shadow picture. The picture even showed her ring! It was the first X-ray picture in history.

TREATING CANCER

In time, scientists found that X-rays damage the cells that make up the human body. This led to the idea that X-rays could be used to destroy a patient's cancer cells. Doctors now bombard diseased cells with X-rays. The X-rays stop the cells from dividing and producing more cells.

CROSS EXAMINATION

CT (Computerized Tomography) is a way of using X-rays to give doctors a cross-section view of the body. A machine aims a thin beam of X-rays at a part of a patient's body from many different angles. The results go into a computer. The computer then builds up a clear 3-D picture of the body part.

GENETIC ENGINEERING

Inventors: Stanley Cohen and Herbert Boyer Year: 1973 Country: United States

THE GENE SCENE

Genes are tiny parts of all living cells. Genes determine the traits that living things inherit from their parents — from the color of a flower to the length of an animal's tail. Genetic engineering replaces or changes genes in a plant or animal to produce desired traits in its offspring. For example, scientists may change the genes in a dog so its puppies will be healthier.

A NEW TOOL

In 1973, Stanley Cohen and Herbert Boyer found a way to change the genes in living things. The scientists replaced genes from one kind of bacteria with genes from another kind of bacteria. As a result, the offspring of the first group of bacteria had the same characteristics as the bacteria in the second group. Cohen and Boyer showed how to use genes to change the offspring of bacteria — or of other living things.

GENE SPLICING

In gene splicing, scientists take a gene from one living thing and join it with a gene in a different living thing. In the early 1960s, scientists used gene splicing to grow corn that tasted better than other corn. Thanks to gene splicing, today's cows give more milk, beef has less fat, and chickens grow faster.

HELLO, DOLLY

A living thing usually starts with cells from two parents. Cloning is a way to grow an animal or plant from a cell of just one parent. The cloned offspring will have the same genes as the one parent. The first clone was a sheep named Dolly, born in Scotland in 1997. Dolly was exactly like its parent in every way. Other labs have cloned very different kinds of animals, from fish to pigs.

FROM LAB TO PATIENT

One of the first tests of human genetic engineering came in 1990. A four-year-old girl had a faulty gene that made her catch many more colds than most people. The doctors removed some white blood cells from the girl's blood and inserted normal genes into the cells. They then put the cells back into her blood. The treatment worked. After that, the girl had fewer colds.

PLASTICS MAKING LIFE EASIER

Inventor: Leo Baekeland Year: 1907 Country: United States

SHAPING UP

Plastic is a man-made material that can be formed into any shape. Workers weave clothes of plastic fibers, make supermarket bags of plastic sheets, and mold bottles, pipes, dishes, chairs, and even auto bodies of solid plastic. Plastics can be as hard as steel or as soft as wool. They can be any color or clear as glass. Plastics can be just about anything people want them to be!

THE FIRST PLASTIC

Leo Baekeland was an American chemist, born in Belgium, who invented plastics by chance. Around 1900, he made a cheap covering to wrap around electric wire. Later he found that if he heated the material, it held its shape. Baekeland named the new substance Bakelite. Before long, he was making everything from pot handles to telephones out of Bakelite — the first practical plastic.

PLASTICS ALL AROUND

Scientists are always looking for new ways to use plastics. Nylon, a kind of plastic, is used to make dresses, tires, fishing line, and auto bodies, among other things. Acrylic, another plastic, is found in carpets, TV screens, airplane windows, and paints. Super-slippery Teflon coats nonstick pots and pans. Super-strong Kevlar is used to make bulletproof vests.

IN PLACE OF

Plastics are rust-free and lighter than iron or steel. Unlike wood, plastics never warp and are easy to clean. Plastics don't break as easily as glass. Plastics take the place of many natural materials. Sometimes it's hard to tell plastic from the real thing!

AFTER THE FACT

The invention of plastics has made life easier and better. But it has also created some problems. Plastics are a major cause of pollution. Most plastics take a very long time to decay or break down. Also, getting rid of plastic waste is very costly. Making new products from recycled plastic is one solution. Another idea is to invent plastics that decay more quickly.

ROBOTS

Inventors: George C. Devol and Joseph F. Engelberger Year: 1956 Country: United States

HARD WORKER

A robot is a machine that does work usually done by humans. Often, the robot does tasks that humans find dangerous, difficult, or unpleasant. Robots make fewer mistakes than humans. They don't need time to rest, eat, or go to the bathroom. In factories, robots do everything from reaching into red-hot furnaces to packing delicate glass in boxes. At home, robots can vacuum a rug without human help.

...ORY ROBOTS

...e C. Devol and Joseph F. ...erger worked together ...o to build a practical ... The robot they made, ..., did not look human ... In fact, it was little more ... a long, strong, metal ... with an electronic "brain." S..., they sold the robot to an auto factory, where it worked on the assembly line.

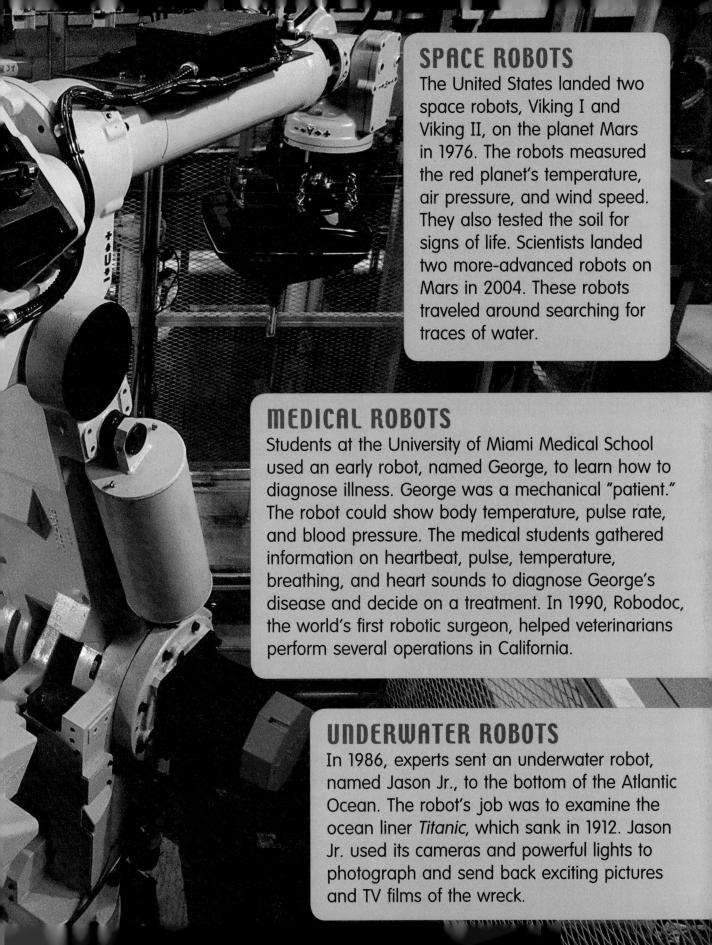

SPACE ROBOTS

The United States landed two space robots, Viking I and Viking II, on the planet Mars in 1976. The robots measured the red planet's temperature, air pressure, and wind speed. They also tested the soil for signs of life. Scientists landed two more-advanced robots on Mars in 2004. These robots traveled around searching for traces of water.

MEDICAL ROBOTS

Students at the University of Miami Medical School used an early robot, named George, to learn how to diagnose illness. George was a mechanical "patient." The robot could show body temperature, pulse rate, and blood pressure. The medical students gathered information on heartbeat, pulse, temperature, breathing, and heart sounds to diagnose George's disease and decide on a treatment. In 1990, Robodoc, the world's first robotic surgeon, helped veterinarians perform several operations in California.

UNDERWATER ROBOTS

In 1986, experts sent an underwater robot, named Jason Jr., to the bottom of the Atlantic Ocean. The robot's job was to examine the ocean liner *Titanic*, which sank in 1912. Jason Jr. used its cameras and powerful lights to photograph and send back exciting pictures and TV films of the wreck.

COPYING MACHINES

Inventor: Chester Carlson Year: 1938 Country: United States

ON THE DOUBLE

In most modern copiers, you put a document into the machine. A bright light shines on it. The light bounces off the original and creates electrical charges on another piece of paper. The machine dusts a fine black powder on the second paper. The powder sticks wherever the words or drawings were reflected. A quick, short burst of heat fixes the powder in place. This makes an exact copy of the document!

ONCE UPON A TIME

Before copying machines, there was no easy way to make copies of handwritten material. President Thomas Jefferson's solution was to write letters with ink that stayed wet for 24 hours. He then pressed a sheet of paper over the original to make a perfect copy — but in reverse. Later, Jefferson got a machine with a second pen attached to his writing pen to make copies. Clearly, there had to be a better way.

CARLSON'S QUEST

In the 1930s, Chester Carlson's job was to make copies of patent applications for the U.S. Patent Office. Poor eyesight and pain in his fingers made it hard to copy the documents by hand. For about eight years, Carlson struggled to invent a machine in which he could "put a paper in a slot and get a copy out." Finally, in 1938, he succeeded in building the first copying machine.

NEW COPIERS

Some recent inventions have improved copying machines. Many copiers now have automatic feeding. If a document has several pages, you stack them all in the machine and let the machine feed them in one at a time. Copiers can reduce or enlarge the size of the copies. Modern copiers can also copy on both sides of a piece of paper.

LATEST COPIERS

The latest copying machines depend on computers. A computer "reads," or scans, the document. It changes everything into computer language and stores the code in its memory. When someone wants a copy of the document, he or she calls up the data from the computer and prints the copy.

AIR CONDITIONERS

Inventor: Willis Carrier Year: 1902 Country: United States

BEAT THE HEAT

An air conditioner helps control the temperature, humidity, dust, and air movement inside a building, car, plane, or train. The basic idea is to keep people cool and comfortable. But air conditioners do more. They remove dirt and dust from the air, keep food fresh in markets, and provide spotless conditions in factories that make drugs or delicate electronic parts.

About 80 percent of all homes in the United States now have air conditioners.

TVs	99%
Ovens	94%
Microwaves	87%
Air Conditioners	80%
Dishwashers	48%

A COOL IDEA

In 1902, a printer in Brooklyn, New York, hired Willis Carrier to help solve a problem. The hot weather made sheets of paper in his printing plant stick together and jam the presses. Carrier designed a machine that pulled in outside air and ran it over pipes filled with cold salt water. The machine then blew the chilled air over the presses. The papers didn't stick — and modern air-conditioning was born!

CLEANS AND BLOWS

Air conditioners also clean the air. Some units force the air through sticky filters that trap most of the dust and dirt in the air. Other filters put an electric charge on the dust and dirt — and capture them electrically.

DRIES AND CHILLS

High temperatures and high humidity make people feel uncomfortable. Modern air conditioners, like Carrier's first one, pass air over cold tubes. The cold chills the air. It also changes the humidity in the air into drops of liquid water. Have you ever seen water dripping from an air conditioner?

MICROWAVE OVENS

Inventor: Percy Spencer Year: 1947 Country: United States

SHORT ORDER

A microwave oven warms or cooks food with very short radio waves, which are called microwaves. These ovens use less energy than regular gas or electric stoves. That's because microwaves cook food very quickly and heat only the food, not the entire unit and the air around it. Also, when prepared in a microwave, many foods keep more of their natural juices.

COOKING WITHOUT GAS

In 1946, Perry Spencer was studying a magnetron — a device that sends out microwaves. One day at work, he put his hand into his pocket and found that his lunchtime chocolate bar had melted. Had the magnetron heated the chocolate? He tried aiming the magnetron at some kernels of popcorn. POP! POP! POP! Sure enough! Spencer had stumbled on a way to cook without gas!

FAST FOOD

Spencer knew that microwaves make the molecules in food shake back and forth, or vibrate, millions of times a second. Vibrating molecules create enough heat to warm or cook food very quickly. So Spencer placed a magnetron inside a metal oven with a small fan to scatter the microwaves. What do you know? Fast cooking had arrived!

BURN OUT

Microwaves can easily pass through glass, china, plastic, or paper dishes or containers. But they cannot pass through metal. Metal bounces back, or reflects, microwaves. In a microwave oven, reflected waves can damage the magnetron. So — never place metal inside a microwave oven!

NO PEEKABOO

The microwave oven is a wonderful invention. But microwaves can be dangerous to humans. Escaping rays can hurt you. They are especially bad for your eyes. The metal mesh in the door is designed to block the rays. But it's best not to get close to a microwave oven — or to sneak a peek inside.

VACUUM CLEANERS

Inventor: Hubert C. Booth Year: 1901 Country: England

QUICK ON THE UPTAKE

A vacuum cleaner sucks up dirt from floors and rugs. Inside the vacuum cleaner is a fast-spinning fan that blows air out of the machine. This creates a partial vacuum. Outside air rushes in to fill the empty space. The rushing air sweeps up nearby dirt. The dirt gets trapped in a cloth or paper bag — and the floor and rugs are left clean.

VROOM!

Hubert C. Booth's 1901 vacuum cleaner was a monster! The machine was so big and heavy that Booth hauled it around London on a horse-drawn wagon. When the wagon pulled up in front of someone's house, workers stretched a long hose through an open window. Then — VROOM — the vacuum cleaner sucked up the dirt in the house!

THE BIG BREAK

Not too many people were interested in Booth's invention at first. People were used to cleaning rugs by beating them with a stick, washing them by hand, or sweeping them with a broom. But in 1902, Booth was asked to clean the red carpet in Westminster Abbey for the coronation of King Edward VII. The public was amazed at how speedily and well the vacuum cleaner worked. Soon people clamored to have their homes cleaned by the new invention.

TOUCH AND GO

No one improved the original vacuum cleaner until 1936. That year, the American William H. Hoover built a much smaller, lighter, upright version that did not need a hose. Also, a spinning brush at the bottom loosened dirt and flung it up into the machine. Before long, almost every home had its own Hoover vacuum cleaner.

THE LAST WORD

Robot vacuum cleaners are the latest thing. They are round, about 14 inches (35.6 cm) wide, and 5.2 inches (13.2 cm) tall. Battery operated and automatic, the robot vacuum cleans rooms, bouncing sounds off the walls and furniture to avoid collisions. But owners must place magnetic strips at doorways to stop the robot from plunging down the stairs!

45

...AND DON'T FORGET

ROLLER BLADES

Every winter, Scott and Brennan Olson played ice hockey. But in the summer, the ice melted. The Olson brothers had to put away their skates. They missed skating in summer until, in 1980, they had a bright idea. They attached a row of roller-skate wheels to a pair of boots. Now they could skate on wheels all summer. The Olsons called their invention Rollerblades.

Inventors: Scott and Brennan Olson
Year: 1980
Country: United States

Inventor: George de Mestral
Year: 1951
Country: Switzerland

VELCRO

One day after a walk in the woods, George de Mestral's jacket was covered with burrs. Curious about what made the burrs stick, de Mestral examined them under a microscope. He saw that the burrs had tiny hooks and the cloth of his jacket had tiny loops. When the hooks caught on the loops, the burrs stuck. De Mestral created two strips of fabric — one with hooks and one with loops. When pressed together, they stuck. He called the system Velcro.

FRISBEES

In the 1870s, students at Yale University used to play catch with metal pie tins. Since the tins came from a pie maker named William Frisbie, the players called the game Frisbie. In 1948, Walter Frederick Morrison and Warren Franscioni made similar disks out of plastic. These disks flew farther and straighter than the old Frisbies. The owner of a toy company later changed the name to Frisbee.

Inventor: Albert J. Parkhouse
Year: 1903
Country: United States

WIRE COAT HANGERS

One day in 1903, Albert Parkhouse showed up for his new job at the Timberlake & Sons company in Jackson, Michigan. He was annoyed that he had no hook on which to hang his coat. So Parkhouse took some wire, looped it around, twisted the ends into a hook, and created a wire coat hanger. Soon the company was making and selling hundreds of Parkhouse's hangers.

Inventor: Walter Frederick Morrison and Warren Franscioni
Year: 1948
Country: United States

BALLPOINT PENS

Before ballpoints, there were only two kinds of pens. Some you dipped in ink and some you filled with ink. Then, in 1938, the brothers Lazlo and Georg Biro invented a completely different kind of pen — the ballpoint. The ink in a ballpoint is as thick as honey. Inside the ballpoint pen, gravity pulls the ink down toward a tiny ball at the tip. As you write, the ball rolls, letting a thin line of ink flow onto the paper. No drip, no mess!

Inventors: Lazlo and Georg Biro
Year: 1938
Country: Hungary

INDEX

A

air conditioners, 5, 7, 40–41
airplanes, 5, 7, 22–23
Altschul, Randice-Lisa, 17
AM (Amplitude Modulation) radio waves, 13
antibiotics, 5, 28–29
automobile, 5, 20–21, 27

B

bacteria, 28, 29, 32
Baekeland, Leo, 34
ballpoint pens, 5, 47
Bardeen, John, 10, 11
Benz, Karl, 20
Biro, Georg and Lazlo, 47
Booth, Hubert C., 44, 45
Boyer, Herbert, 32
Brattain, Walter, 10, 11

C

cancer, 31
Carlson, Chester, 38
Carrier, Willis, 40, 41
cars, see automobiles
CDs, 18–19
cell phones, 16–17
clone, genetic, 33
Cohen, Stanley, 32
computers, 6–7, 9, 10, 19, 39
Cooper, Martin, 16, 17
copying machines, 38–39
CT (Computerized Tomography), 31

D

Daimler, Gottlieb, 20
data, 6, 7, 9, 19, 39
da Vinci, Leonardo, 22
de Mestral, George, 46
Devol, George C., 36
Dolly (cloned sheep), 33
DVDs, 19

E

Eckert, Jr., J. Presper, 6
electricity, 10, 11, 19, 21
Engelberger, Joseph F., 36
ENIAC (Electronic Numerical Integrator And Computer), 6

F

Faraday, Michael, 13
fiber-optic cable, 9
fireworks, 26, 27
Fleming, Alexander, 28, 29
flight, mechanics of, 22, 23, 24
FM (Frequency Modulation) radio waves, 13
Focke, Heinrich, 24
food, 42, 43
Ford, Henry, 20
Franscioni, Warren, 47
Frisbees, 5, 47

G

gasoline, 20, 21, 27
gene splicing, 33
genetic engineering, 32–33
George (medical robot), 37
germs, 28, 29
Goddard, Robert, 26, 27

H

helicopters, 5, 24–25
Henry, Joseph, 13
HDTV (High Definition TeleVision), 15
Hoover, William H., 45
hybrid cars, 21

J

Jason Jr. (underwater robot), 37
Jefferson, Thomas (U.S. president), 38

K

Kevlar, 35

L

lasers, 8–9, 19
livestock, genetic engineering, 33

M

magnetron, 42, 43
Maiman, Theodore H., 8, 9
Marconi, Guglielmo, 12, 13
Mauchly, John William, 6
medical robots, 37
microphones, 12, 14, 19
microwave ovens, 5, 7, 42–43
Morrison, Walter Frederick, 47
music, 15, 18

N

nylon, 35

O

Olson, Brennan and Scott, 46

P

Pall, Teri, 17
Parkhouse, Albert J., 47
penicillin, 29
pens, see ballpoint pens
plastics, 5, 34–35

R

radio, 5, 11, 12–13
waves, 12, 13, 14, 42
recycled plastic, 35
Reitsch, Hanna, 24
Robodoc (robotic surgeon), 37
robots, 36–37, 45
robot vacuum cleaners, 45
rockets, 5, 26–27
Roentgen, Wilhelm Conrad, 30, 31
Rollerblades, 5, 46
Russell, James T., 18

S

satellites, 7, 14, 15, 27
satellite television, 15
Shockley, William, 10, 11
Sikorsky, Igor, 24
space (outer), 26, 37
Spencer, Percy, 42–43
surgery, eye, 9

T

Teflon, 35
television, 5, 7, 10, 14–15
invention of, 15
programs, 9, 15
transistors, 10–11
travel, world of 1900, 5

U

underwater robots, 37
United States
air-conditioner usage,
appliance usage, 40
cell phone users, 17
space travel, 26

V

vacuum cleaners, 5, 44–45
Velcro, 5, 46
video cameras, 7
Viking I and Viking II (space robots), 37
viruses, 29

W

weapons, army, 6
wire coat hangers, 5, 47
Wright, Orville and Wilbur, 22, 23

X

X-rays, 30–31

Z

Zworykin, Vladimir K., 14,